AMERICAN
WIT AND WISDOM

AMERICAN WIT AND WISDOM

Selected by
REV. JAMES L. DOW, M.A.

Illustrated by Val Biro

COLLINS London and Glasgow

General Editor: W. T. McLeod
First published 1971

ISBN 0 00 410320 3
Copyright 1971
William Collins Sons and Company Limited
Printed in Great Britain
by Collins Clear-Type Press

CONTENTS

INTRODUCTION

Most people have some favourite quotations and the first thing they do when they open an anthology is to look for them. The anthology often stands condemned if the quotation is not included.

This is not meant to be a comprehensive catalogue of all the wise things that Americans have said. These are just passages that have interested me; which I have noted on the back pages of books, put into commonplace books, and used in writing. There are nearly 500 quotations here, from about 65 authors. Some writers appear more often than others, for the simple reason that they wrote more and are more quotable. At least half a dozen of them would need anthologies to themselves to do them justice.

Arrangement was a problem, until I remembered Shakespeare, who is part of the American tradition. They say that American English is closer to Shakespeare's English than English English is. Being a Scotsman, I wouldn't know. The pattern of this small volume will be found in this Shakespearean quotation:

And one man in his time plays many parts,
His acts being seven ages. At first the infant,
Mewling and puking in the nurse's arms.
And then the whining schoolboy, with his satchel

And shining morning face, creeping like snail
Unwillingly to school. And then the lover,
Sighing like furnace, with a woeful ballad
Made to his mistress' eyebrow. Then a soldier,
Full of strange oaths, and bearded like the pard,
Jealous in honour, sudden and quick in quarrel,
Seeking the bubble reputation
Even in the cannon's mouth. And then the justice,
In fair round belly with good capon lin'd,
With eyes severe and beard of formal cut,
Full of wise saws and modern instances;
And so he plays his part. The sixth age shifts
Into the lean and slipper'd pantaloon,
With spectacles on nose and pouch on side,
His youthful hose, well sav'd, a world too wide
For his shrunk shank; and his big manly voice,
Turning again towards childish treble, pipes
And whistles in his sound. Last scene of all,
That ends this strange eventful history,
Is second childishness, and mere oblivion;
Sans teeth, sans eyes, sans taste, sans everything.

THE INFANT

We are born believing. A man bears beliefs as a tree
bears apples.   RALPH WALDO EMERSON

★★★

The cat, having sat on a hot stove lid, will not sit on
a hot stove lid again. Nor upon a cold stove lid.
                                        MARK TWAIN

★★★

The burnt child shuns the fire until next day.
                                        MARK TWAIN

★★★

Teach your child to hold his tongue; he'll learn
fast enough to speak.   BENJAMIN FRANKLIN

★★★

'Who was your mother?' 'Never had none', said
the child with another grin. 'Never had any
mother? What do you mean? Where were you
born?' 'Never was born', persisted Topsy . . . 'I
'spect I growed.'   HARRIET BEECHER STOWE

★★★

A sleeping child gives me the impression of a
traveller in a very far country.
                            RALPH WALDO EMERSON

There are two things in life for which we are never
fully prepared; and that is twins.   JOSH BILLINGS

O great Creator, why was our Nature
    depraved and forlorn?
Why so defil'd and made so wild
    whilst we were yet unborn?
If it be just, and needs we must
    transgressors reckoned be,
Thy Mercy, Lord, to us afford,
    which sinners hath set free.
                        MICHAEL WIGGLESWORTH

Not only around our infancy
Doth heaven with all its splendours lie;
Daily, with souls that cringe and plot,
We Sinais climb and know it not.
                        JAMES RUSSELL LOWELL

THE SCHOOLBOY

But by and by she let out that Moses had been dead a very long time: so then I didn't care no more about him. Because I don't take no stock in dead people.   MARK TWAIN

The opening of the first grammar school was the opening of the first trench against monopoly in church and state; the first row of trammels and pothooks which the little Shearjashubs and Elk-anahs blotted and blubbered across their copy-books was the preamble to the Declaration of Independence.   JAMES RUSSELL LOWELL

Wisdom never made a bigot, but learning has.
                                        JOSH BILLINGS

I not only use all the brains I have, but all I can borrow.   JOSH BILLINGS

When I was a boy of fourteen my father was so ignorant I could hardly stand to have the old man around. But when I got to twenty one I was astonished at what he had learned in seven years.
                                        MARK TWAIN

A classic is something that everybody wants to have
read, and nobody wants to read.   MARK TWAIN

There are those who scoff at the schoolboy,
calling him frivolous and shallow. Yet it was a
schoolboy who said '*Faith* is believing what you
know ain't so'.   MARK TWAIN

He who knows nothing is nearer the truth than he
whose mind is filled with falsehoods and errors.
                              THOMAS JEFFERSON

How dear to this heart are the scenes of my
    childhood,
When fond recollection presents them to view.
The orchard, the meadow, the deep tangled
    wildwood,
And every loved spot which my infancy knew.
The wide spreading pond and the mill that
    stood by it,
The bridge and the rock where the cataract fell,
The cot of my father, the dairy house nigh it,
And e'en the rude bucket that hung in the well.
The old oaken bucket, the iron-bound bucket,
The moss-covered bucket which hung in the well.
                          SAMUEL WOODWORTH

The mountain and the squirrel
Had a quarrel,
And the former called the latter 'Little Prig';
Bun replied,
'You are doubtless very big;
But all sorts of things and weather
Must be taken in together,
To make up a year,
And a sphere.
And I think it no disgrace
To occupy my place.
If I am not so large as you,
You are not so small as I,
And not half so spry.
I'll not deny you'll make
A very pretty squirrel track;
Talents differ; all is well and wisely put;
If I cannot carry forests on my back,
Neither can you crack a nut.'

RALPH WALDO EMERSON

To bring up a child in the way he should go,
travel that way yourself once in a while.

JOSH BILLINGS

So nigh is grandeur to our dust,
So nigh is God to man,
When duty whispers low, *Thou must*;
The youth replies, *I can.* RALPH WALDO EMERSON

When I was a boy I'd rather be licked once than postponed twice.   JOSH BILLINGS

Training is everything. The peach was once a bitter almond; cauliflower is but cabbage with a college education.   MARK TWAIN

The gases gather to the solid firmament; the chemic lump arrives at the plant and grows; arrives at the quadruped and walks; arrives at the man, and thinks.   RALPH WALDO EMERSON

Work as if you were to live one hundred years; pray as if you were to die tomorrow.
                    RALPH WALDO EMERSON

Sammy is a well of truth, but you can't bring it all up in one bucket.   MRS CLEMENS

A boy's will is the wind's will,
And the thoughts of youth are long, long thoughts.
                    HENRY WADSWORTH LONGFELLOW

I'd rather be a bright-haired boy
Than reign a gray-beard king.

RALPH WALDO EMERSON

Silence! The second class must read.
As quick as possible proceed.
Not found your books yet? Stand, be fixed.
The next read. Stop—the next—the next.
You need not read again, 'tis well.
Come, Tom and Dick, choose sides to spell.
Will this word do? Yes, Tom, spell *dunce*.
Sit still there all you little ones.
I've got a word. Well, name it. *Gizzard*.
You spell it, Sampson. G I Z izzard.
Spell conscience, Jack. K O N S H U N T S.
Well done!
Pull out the next. Mine is *folks*.
Tim, spell it. P H O U X.

O shocking! Have you all try'd? No.
Say *Master*, but no matter, go . . .
Lay by your books; and you, Josiah,
Help Jed to make the morning fire.   ANONYMOUS

How can I teach your children gentleness,
    And mercy to the weak, and reverence
For Life, which, in its weakness or excess,
    Is still a gleam of God's omnipotence,

Or Death, which seeming darkness, is no less
  The selfsame light, although averted hence,
When by your laws, your actions, and your speech,
You contradict the very things I teach?
                    HENRY WADSWORTH LONGFELLOW

★★★

When I heard the learn'd astronomer,
When the proofs, the figures, were ranged in
    columns before me,
When I was shown the charts and diagrams, to
    add, divide, and measure them,
When I sitting heard the astronomer where
    he lectured with much applause in the
    lecture room,
How soon unaccountable I became tired and sick,
Till rising and gliding out I wander'd off by
    myself,
In the mystical moist night-air, and from time to
    time,
Look'd up in perfect silence at the stars.
                    WALT WHITMAN

★★★

Little David, play on yo' harp,
Hallelujah, Hallelujah.
Little David, play on yo' harp,
Hallelujah.

Little David was a shepherd boy,
He killed Goliath an' he shouted for joy.

Joshua was de son of Nun,
He never quit till his work was done.

Done told you once, done told you twice,
You can't get to heaven by a-rollin' of dice.

Little David, play on yo' harp,
Hallelujah, Hallelujah.
Little David, play on yo' harp,
Hallelujah. SPIRITUAL

★★★

    . . . as he hears
From the gray dame the tales of other years;
. . . And then the chubby grand-child wants to
    know
About the ghosts and witches long ago,
That haunted the old swamp.
    The clock strikes ten——
The prayer is said, nor unforgotten then
The stranger in their gates. A decent rule
Of Elders in thy Puritanic school.
JOHN G. C. BRAINARD

★★★

Education should not confine itself to books. It
must train executive power, and try to create that
right public opinion which is the most potent
factor in the proper solution of all political and
social questions. Book-learning is very important,
but it is by no means everything.
THEODORE ROOSEVELT

Education makes a greater difference between man and man than nature has made between man and brute.   JOHN ADAMS

A well instructed people alone can be permanently a free people.   JAMES MADISON

It is hard to fail; but it is worse never to have tried to succeed.   THEODORE ROOSEVELT

The free man cannot be long an ignorant man.
                                   WILLIAM MCKINLEY

I am happiest when I am idle. I could live for months without performing any kind of labor, and at the expiration of that time I should feel fresh and vigorous enough to go right on in the same way for numerous more months.
                                        ARTEMUS WARD

The college has konfered upon me the honerery title of T.K., of which I am sufishuntly prowd.
                                        ARTEMUS WARD

When I was a beggarly boy,
  And lived in a cellar damp,
I had not a friend nor a toy,
  But I had Aladdin's lamp;
When I could not sleep for the cold,
  I had fire enough in my brain,
And builded with roofs of gold,
  My beautiful castles in Spain.

Since then I have toiled day and night,
  I have money and power good store,
But I'd give all my lamps of silver bright,
  For the one that is mine no more;
Take, Fortune, whatever you choose,
  You gave, and may snatch again;
I have nothing 'twould pain me to lose,
  For I own no more castles in Spain.

JAMES RUSSELL LOWELL

★★★

The commonplace I sing;
How cheap is health! How cheap nobility!
Abstinence, no falsehood, no gluttony, lust;
The open air I sing, freedom, toleration,
(Take here the mainest lesson, less from books,
    less from the schools)
The common day and night, the common earth
    and waters,
Your farm, your work, trade, occupation,
The democratic wisdom underneath, like solid
    ground for all.

WALT WHITMAN

The human mind is full of curiosity but it don't
love to be taught.   JOSH BILLINGS

★★★

To be good is noble, but to teach others how to be
good is nobler—and less trouble.   MARK TWAIN

★★★

George Washington was ignorant of the common-
est accomplishments of youth. He could not even
lie.   MARK TWAIN

★★★

Have a place for everything and keep the thing
somewhere else; this is not advice, it is merely
custom.   MARK TWAIN

★★★

A learned fool is one who has read everything and
remembered it.   JOSH BILLINGS

★★★

Genius learns from nature; talent from books.
        JOSH BILLINGS

★★★

To inherit property is not to be born—it is to be
still-born.   HENRY DAVID THOREAU

Don't part with your illusions. When they are gone you may still exist, but you have ceased to live.   MARK TWAIN

Life consists not in holding good cards, but in playing those you do hold well.   JOSH BILLINGS

The things taught in colleges and schools are not an education, but the means of education.

RALPH WALDO EMERSON

A child thinks twenty shillings and twenty years can scarce ever be spent.   BENJAMIN FRANKLIN

People born to be hanged are safe in water.

MARK TWAIN

Meek young men grow up in libraries believing it their duty to accept the views which Cicero, which Locke, which Bacon have given; forgetful that Cicero, Locke and Bacon were only young men in libraries when they wrote these books.

RALPH WALDO EMERSON

Our chief want in life is somebody who shall make us do what we can.   RALPH WALDO EMERSON

If a man could have half his wishes he would double his troubles.   BENJAMIN FRANKLIN

Those who work much do not work hard.
HENRY DAVID THOREAU

★★★

Write without pay until somebody offers pay. If nobody offers within three years the candidate may look upon this circumstance with the most implicit confidence as the sign that sawing wood is what he was intended for.   MARK TWAIN

★★★

Old boys have their playthings as well as the young ones. The difference is only the price.
BENJAMIN FRANKLIN

★★★

Consider the postage stamp: its usefulness consists in the ability to stick to one thing until it gets there.   JOSH BILLINGS

Success has ruined many a man.

BENJAMIN FRANKLIN

Water-Boy, where are yo' hidin'?
If yo' don't-a come, gwine tell-a yo' Mammy.

Dere ain't no hammer dat's on-a dis mountain,
Dat ring-a like mine, boys, dat ring-a like mine.
Done bus' dis rock, boys, from heah to Macon,
Right back to de jail, boys, right back to de jail.

Yo' Jack o' Dimon's, yo' Jack o' Dimon's,
I know yo' of old, boys, I know yo' of old.
You rob-a ma pocket, yas, rob-a ma pocket,
Done rob-a ma pocket of silver an' gold.

Water-Boy, where are yo' hidin'?
If you don't-a come, gwine tell-a yo' Mammy.

TRADITIONAL

There was a little girl
Who had a little curl
Right in the middle of her forehead.
When she was good
She was very very good,
But when she was bad she was horrid.

HENRY WADSWORTH LONGFELLOW

You've a darned long row to hoe.

JAMES RUSSELL LOWELL

Men are generally more careful of the breed of their horses and dogs than of their children.

WILLIAM PENN

Hitch your wagon to a star.

RALPH WALDO EMERSON

THE LOVER

If you have built castles in the air, your work need not be lost; that is where they should be. Now put the foundations under them.

HENRY DAVID THOREAU

Money will buy a pretty dog, but it won't buy a wag of its tail.

JOSH BILLINGS

There are people who can do all fine and heroic things but one; keep from telling their happiness to the unhappy.

MARK TWAIN

Those whom we love we can hate; to others we are indifferent.

HENRY DAVID THOREAU

Grief can take care of itself, but to get the full value of a joy you must have somebody to divide it with.

MARK TWAIN

Some of your griefs you have cured,
  And the sharpest you still have survived;
But what torments of pain you endured
  From the evils that never arrived.

RALPH WALDO EMERSON

Though thou loved her as thyself,
As a self of purer clay,
Though her parting dims the day,
Stealing grace from all alive;
Heartily know,
When half gods go,
The gods arrive.   RALPH WALDO EMERSON

Love is the torment of one, the felicity of two, the
strife and enmity of three.   WASHINGTON IRVING

Look out upon the stars my love,
    And shame them with thine eyes,
On which, than on the lights above,
    There hang more destinies.
Night's beauty is the harmony
    Of blending shades and lights
Then, lady, up—look out and be
    A sister to the night.   EDWARD COOTE PINKNEY

Give all to love;
Obey thy heart;
Friends, kindred, days,
Estate, good fame,
Plans, credit and the Muse—
Nothing refuse.   RALPH WALDO EMERSON

Her health! and would on earth there stood,
  Some more of such a frame,
That life might be all poetry,
  And weariness a name.

EDWARD COOTE PINKNEY

★★★

Hast thou named all the birds without a gun?
Loved the wood rose and left it on its stalk?
At rich men's tables eaten bread and pulse?
Unarmed, faced danger with heart of trust?
And loved so well a high behaviour
In man or maid, that thou from speech refrained
Nobility more nobly to repay?
O, be my friend, and teach me to be thine!

RALPH WALDO EMERSON

★★★

The turtle on yon withered bough,
  That lately mourned her murdered mate,
Has found another comrade now—
  Such changes all await!
Again her drooping plume is drest,
Again she's willing to be blest
And takes her lover to her nest.

If nature has decreed it so
With all above, and all below,
Let us like them forget our woe,
  And not be killed with sorrow.
If I should quit your arms tonight

A.W.W—B.

And chance to die before 'twas light,
I would advise you—and you might—
   Love again tomorrow.
               PHILIP FRENEAU

★★★

Be wise then, ye maidens, nor seek admiration
By dressing for conquest, and flirting with all;
You never, whatever your fortune or station,
Appear half so lovely at rout or at ball,
As gaily convened at a work covered table,
Each cheerfully active and playing her part,
Beguiling the task with a song or a fable,
And plying her needle with exquisite art.
The bright little needle, the swift flying needle,
The needle directed by beauty and art.
               SAMUEL WOODWORTH

★★★

'Only a housemaid!' She looked from the kitchen,
   Neat was the kitchen and tidy was she;
There at the window a sempstress sat stitching;
   'Were I a sempstress, how happy I'd be!'

'Only a Queen!' She looked over the waters,
   Fair was her kingdom, and mighty was she;
There sat an Empress, with Queens for her
      daughters;
   'Were I an Empress, how happy I'd be!'

Still the old frailty they all of them trip in!
   Eve in her daughters is ever the same;

Give her all Eden, she sighs for a pippin;
  Give her an Empire, she pined for a name.
                              OLIVER WENDELL HOLMES

★★★

Helen, thy beauty is to me
  Like those Nicean barks of yore,
That gently, o'er a perfumed sea,
  The weary, way-worn wanderer bore
  To his own native shore.   EDGAR ALLAN POE

★★★

Thou wouldst be loved? Then let thy heart
  From its present pathway part not.
Being everything which now thou art,
  Be nothing which thou art not.
So with the world thy gentle ways,
  Thy grace, thy more than beauty,
Shall be an endless theme of praise,
  And love—a simple duty.   EDGAR ALLAN POE

★★★

Alas, she married another; they frequently do. I
hope she is happy, because I am. ARTEMUS WARD

★★★

'God bless the man who first invented sleep!'
  So Sancho Panza said, and so say I:
And bless him also, that he didn't keep

His great discovery to himself; nor try
To make it, as the lucky fellow might,
    A close monopoly by patent right.

The time for honest folks to be a-bed
    Is in the morning, if I reason right;
And he who cannot keep his precious head
    Upon his pillow till it's fairly light,
And so enjoy his forty morning winks,
    Is up to knavery—or else he drinks.
                                    JOHN G. SAXE

★★★

The earth, that is sufficient,
I do not want the constellations any nearer,
I know they are very well where they are,
I know they suffice for those who belong to them.
                                    WALT WHITMAN

★★★

Missus marry Will de weaber;
William was a gay deceaber;
When he put his arm around 'er,
He looked as fierce as a forty-pounder.
While missus libbed, she libbed in clober,
When she died, she died all ober;
How could she act de foolish part,
An' marry a man to break her heart?
                                    DANIEL D. EMMET

She laughs at everything you say. Why? Because she has fine teeth. BENJAMIN FRANKLIN

Keep your eyes wide open before marriage, and half shut afterwards. BENJAMIN FRANKLIN

What, sir, would the people of the earth be without woman? They would be scarce, sir, almighty scarce. MARK TWAIN

To find out a girl's faults, praise her to her girl friends. BENJAMIN FRANKLIN

When women cease to be handsome they study to be good. To maintain their influence over men, they supply the diminution of beauty by the augmentation of utility. They learn to do a thousand services small and great, and are the most tender and useful of friends when you are sick. Thus they continue amiable. And hence there is hardly such a thing to be found as an old woman who is not a good woman.

BENJAMIN FRANKLIN

The happy married man dies in good stile at home, surrounded by his weeping wife and children. The old bachelor don't die at all—he sort of rots away like a pollywog's tail.   ARTEMUS WARD

If you mean getting hitched, *I'm in.*

ARTEMUS WARD

Once in an age God sends to some of us a friend who loves us; not a false imagining, an unreal character—but, looking through all the rubbish of our imperfections, loves in us the divine ideal of our nature—loves not the man that we are, but the angel that we may be.   HARRIET BEECHER STOWE

Many a man thinks he's buying a pleasure, when he's really selling himself a slave to it.

BENJAMIN FRANKLIN

A single man has not nearly the value he would have in the state of union. He is an incomplete animal. He resembles the odd half of a pair of scissors.   BENJAMIN FRANKLIN

Tell me how much one loves, and I will tell you
how much he has seen of God.

HENRY DAVID THOREAU

Laugh and the world laughs with you;
Weep and you weep alone;
For sad old earth must borrow its mirth,
But has trouble enough of its own.

ELLA WHEELER WILCOX

All mankind loves a lover.

RALPH WALDO EMERSON

The men that women marry, and why they marry
them will always be a marvel and a mystery to the
world.   HENRY WADSWORTH LONGFELLOW

Talk not of wasted affection, affection never was
wasted.   HENRY WADSWORTH LONGFELLOW

Most folks are about as happy as they make up their
minds to be.   ABRAHAM LINCOLN

When I was a young man I courted popularity. I found her but a coy mistress, and I soon deserted her. Our ancestors, the Puritans, were a most unpopular set of men; yet the world owes all the liberty it possesses to them.   JOHN ADAMS

★★★

Associate yourself with men of good quality if you esteem your own reputation; for it is better to be alone than in bad company.

GEORGE WASHINGTON

★★★

Nothing gives one person so much advantage over another as to remain always cool and unruffled under any circumstances.   THOMAS JEFFERSON

★★★

Poets may be born, but success is made.

JAMES A. GARFIELD

★★★

Nine-tenths of wisdom is being wise in time.

THEODORE ROOSEVELT

★★★

A woman is the only thing that I am afraid of that I know will not hurt me.   ABRAHAM LINCOLN

There is a time to wink as well as to see.

BENJAMIN FRANKLIN

One half of the troubles of this life can be traced to saying *yes* too quick and not saying *no* soon enough.

JOSH BILLINGS

Marie Antoinette is devoted to pleasure and expense and is not remarkable for any other vices or virtues.

THOMAS JEFFERSON

It is much easier to repent of sins that we have committed than to repent of those we intend to commit.

JOSH BILLINGS

Love is like measles: you can get it only once, and the later in life it occurs the tougher it gets.

JOSH BILLINGS

Friendship is like earthenware, once broken it can be mended; love is like a mirror, once broken that ends it.

JOSH BILLINGS

Nothing is better than simplicity. WALT WHITMAN

***

The female woman is one of the greatest institoo-
shuns of which this land can boste.
ARTEMUS WARD

***

'I wish thar was winders to my sole', sed I, 'so that
you could see some of my feelins.' ARTEMUS WARD

***

Life is action; the use of one's powers.
OLIVER WENDELL HOLMES

***

Water, taken in moderation, cannot hurt anybody.
MARK TWAIN

***

There are people so addicted to exaggeration that
they can't tell the truth without lying.
JOSH BILLINGS

***

The hardest sinner in the whole lot to convert is the
one who spends half his time sinning and the other
half in repentance. JOSH BILLINGS

THE SOLDIER

With the dreadful strain of war upon me, if I did not laugh I should die.   ABRAHAM LINCOLN

My dear McLellan, if you do not want to use the army I should like to borrow it for a while.

    ABRAHAM LINCOLN

'But surely you must admit, Mr President, that no scholar of our generation has plunged more deeply into the fount of learning.' 'Yes', said LINCOLN, 'or come up drier.'

'Abe, that was a right smart speech, but there were some things you said that were outside my reach.' 'I'm sorry to hear that,' said LINCOLN. 'I once had a dog that had the same trouble with fleas.'

No man has a good enough memory to be a successful liar.   ABRAHAM LINCOLN

The street called Straight is straighter than a corkscrew, but not as straight as a rainbow.

    MARK TWAIN

He who would invade the sanctities of his mother tongue would invade the recesses of the paternal till without remorse.   OLIVER WENDELL HOLMES

At the same time he let off one of those big words which lie at the bottom of the best man's vocabulary, but perhaps never turn up in his life—just as every man's hair may stand on end, but in most men it never does.   OLIVER WENDELL HOLMES

Put none but Americans on guard tonight.
GEORGE WASHINGTON

When angry, count ten before you speak; if very angry, an hundred.   THOMAS JEFFERSON

A fellow once came to me to ask for an appointment as a minister abroad. Finding he could not get that, he came down to a more modest position. Finally he asked to be made a tide-waiter. When he saw he could not get that, he asked me for an old pair of trousers. It is sometimes well to be humble.   ABRAHAM LINCOLN

Disarmament can never be of prime importance; there is more need to get rid of the causes of war than of the implements of war.

THEODORE ROOSEVELT

★★★

We Americans have no commission from God to police the world.   BENJAMIN HARRISON

I would to God we had less professions and more acts of real patriotism.   ANDREW JACKSON

To be prepared for war is one of the most effective ways of preserving peace.   GEORGE WASHINGTON

★★★

Witness the cider barrel, the log cabin, the hickory stick, the palmetto and all the cognizances of party. See the power of national emblems. Some stars, lilies, leopards, a crescent, a lion, an eagle, or other figure which came into credit, God knows how, an old rag of bunting blowing in the wind, on a fort, at the ends of the earth, shall make the blood tingle under the rudest or the most conventional exterior. The people fancy they hate poetry, and they are all poets and mystics! . . . For we are not pans and barrows, nor even porters of the fire and torch

bearers, but children of the fire, made of it, and
only the same divinity transmuted.

RALPH WALDO EMERSON

★★★

Were half the power that fills the world with
    terror,
  Were half the wealth bestowed on camps and
    courts,
Given to redeem the human mind from error,
  There were no need of arsenals and forts.

HENRY WADSWORTH LONGFELLOW

★★★

And the night shall be filled with music,
  And the cares that infest the day,
Shall fold their tents, like the Arabs,
  And as silently steal away.

HENRY WADSWORTH LONGFELLOW

★★★

You may talk about yo' King ob Gideon,
You may talk about yo' man ob Saul,
Dere's none like good ole Joshua,
At de battle ob Jerico.
Dat mornin'——
Joshua fit de battle ob Jerico—Jerico—Jerico,
Joshua fit de battle ob Jerico,
An' de walls came a-tumbelin' down.   SPIRITUAL

With Freedom's soil beneath our feet,
And Freedom's banner streaming o'er us.

JOSEPH RODMAN DRAKE

Bravest of all in Frederick town,
She took up the flag the men hauled down.

JOHN GREENLEAF WHITTIER

I also say it is good to fail. Battles are lost in the
same spirit in which they are won.

WALT WHITMAN

A hero is no braver than an ordinary man, but he
is brave five minutes longer.

RALPH WALDO EMERSON

A great part of courage is the courage of having
done the thing before.   RALPH WALDO EMERSON

One thing is clear. Before lasting peace can be
restored much must be forgiven, if not forgotten.

MILLARD FILLMORE

Each generation should be made to bear the burden of its own wars, instead of carrying them on at the expense of other generations.

JAMES MADISON

No man can be a good citizen unless he has a wage more than sufficient to cover the bare cost of living, and hours of labor short enough so that after his day's work is done he will have time and energy enough to bear his share in the management of the community; to help in carrying the general load.   THEODORE ROOSEVELT

Is there anything in it glorious and dear for a nation, that is not also glorious and dear for a man? What is freedom to a nation but freedom to the individuals in it?   HARRIET BEECHER STOWE

It were better to be of no church than to be bitter for any.   BENJAMIN FRANKLIN

Noise proves nothing. Often a hen who has merely laid an egg cackles as if she had laid an asteroid.

MARK TWAIN

There are several good protections against temptation, but the surest is cowardice.   MARK TWAIN

The man who has never been tempted doesn't know how dishonest he is.   JOSH BILLINGS

For He that worketh high and wise,
  Nor pauses in His plan,
Will take the sun out of the skies
  Ere freedom out of man.

RALPH WALDO EMERSON

Clean your fingers before you point at my spots.

BENJAMIN FRANKLIN

I don't know who my grandfather was, and I am much more concerned to know what his grandson will be.   ABRAHAM LINCOLN

'What, Mr President, do you black your own shoes?' 'Yes,' says LINCOLN, 'whose do you black?'

Other misfortunes may be borne, or their effects overcome. If disastrous war should sweep our commerce from the ocean, another generation may renew it; if it exhausts our treasury, future industry may replenish it; if it desolate and lay waste our fields, still, under a new cultivation, they will grow green again and ripen to future harvests. It were but a trifle if the walls of yonder Capitol were to crumble and its lofty pillars should fall, and its gorgeous decorations be all covered by the dust of the valley. All these might be rebuilt. But who shall reconstruct the fabric of demolished government? Who shall rear again the well-proportioned columns of constitutional liberty: who shall frame together the skilful architecture which unites national sovereignty with State rights, individual security and public prosperity?   DANIEL WEBSTER

Be sure you are right. Then go ahead.

DAVY CROCKETT

We do not quite forgive a giver.

RALPH WALDO EMERSON

Let us have faith that Right makes Might, and in that faith let us to the end dare to do our duty as we understand it.   ABRAHAM LINCOLN

Whoso would be a man must be a nonconformist. Nothing is at last sacred but the integrity of your own mind.   RALPH WALDO EMERSON

Towering genius disdains a beaten path. It seeks regions hitherto unexplored.   ABRAHAM LINCOLN

Sin has many tools, but a lie is the handle that fits them all.   OLIVER WENDELL HOLMES

I find the great thing in this world is not so much where we stand as in what direction we are moving. To reach the port of heaven we must sail sometimes with the wind and sometimes against it—but we must sail, and not drift nor lie at anchor.

OLIVER WENDELL HOLMES

The undisciplined mind is far better adapted to the confused world in which we live today, than the streamlined mind.   HENRY DAVID THOREAU

To the discontented man no chair is easy.

BENJAMIN FRANKLIN

The truly wise man or woman will recognise no one as an enemy. You can pay him in his own coin. If you do this you will get even with him by sinking yourself to his level, and both of you will suffer by it.   HENRY DAVID THOREAU

The best creed we can have is charity towards the creeds of others.   JOSH BILLINGS

Those who enter heaven may find the outer walls plastered with creeds but they won't find any on the inside.   JOSH BILLINGS

If the desire to kill and the opportunity to kill came always together, who would escape hanging?
                    MARK TWAIN

I was gratified to be able to answer properly, and I did. I said I didn't know.   MARK TWAIN

I once heard a preacher who was powerful good. I decided to give him every cent I had with me. But he kept at it too long. Ten minutes later I decided to keep the bills and just give him my loose change.

Another ten minutes and I was darned if I would give him anything at all. Then when he finally stopped and the plate came round I was so exhausted I extracted two dollars out of sheer spite.

MARK TWAIN

Men lose their tempers in defending their taste.

RALPH WALDO EMERSON

If you tell the truth you don't have to remember anything.   MARK TWAIN

In every work of genius we recognise our own rejected thoughts; they come back to us with a certain alienated majesty. RALPH WALDO EMERSON

Truth is stranger than fiction, because fiction is obliged to stick to possibilities: truth isn't.

MARK TWAIN

To believe your own thought; to believe that what is true for you in your private heart is true for all men—that is genius.   RALPH WALDO EMERSON

My countrymen, one and all, think calmly and well upon this whole subject. Nothing valuable can be lost by taking time. If there be an object to hurry any of you in hot haste to a step which you would never take deliberately, that object will be frustrated by taking time: but no good object can be frustrated by it.   ABRAHAM LINCOLN

If you would win a man to your cause first convince him that you are his sincere friend.

ABRAHAM LINCOLN

I was just going to say when I was interrupted...
OLIVER WENDELL HOLMES

There are some men that it weakens one to talk with an hour, more than a day's fasting would do.
OLIVER WENDELL HOLMES

A pun does not commonly justify a blow in return. But if a blow were given for such a cause, and death ensued, the jury would be judges both of the facts and of the pun, and might, if the latter were of an aggravated character, return a verdict of justifiable homicide.   OLIVER WENDELL HOLMES

If the windows of your soul are dirty and streaked, covered with matter foreign to them, then the world as you look out of them, will be to you dirty and streaked and out of order.

HENRY DAVID THOREAU

The mean mechanic finds his kindly rest,
All void of fear sleepeth the Country-Clown,
When greatest princes often are distressed
And cannot sleep upon their Beds of Down.

MICHAEL WIGGLESWORTH

It was on a Wednesday night, the moon was
    shining bright,
  They robbed the Danville train.
And the people they did say, for many miles
    away,
  'Twas the outlaws, Frank and Jesse James.

Jesse had a wife to mourn him all her life,
  The children they are brave.
'Twas a dirty little coward shot Mister Howard,
  And laid Jesse James in his grave.

Jesse went to rest with his hand on his breast;
  And he died with a smile on his face.
He was born one day in the county of Clay,
  And he came from a solitary race.

COWBOY BALLAD

Hatred, envy, malice, jealousy and revenge, all have children. Every bad thought breeds others, and each of these goes on and on, ever reproducing itself, until our world is peopled with their off-spring.   HENRY DAVID THOREAU

We boil at different degrees.
                    RALPH WALDO EMERSON

Let thy discontents be secret.
                    BENJAMIN FRANKLIN

Whist has been noted for its influence upon what is termed the calculating power; and men of the highest order of intellect have been known to take an apparently unaccountable delight in it, while eschewing chess as frivolous. . . . The best player of chess in Christendom may be little more than the best player of chess; but proficiency in whist implies capacity for success in all these more important undertakings where mind struggles with mind.   EDGAR ALLEN POE

What a good thing Adam had—when he said a good thing he knew nobody had said it before.
                    MARK TWAIN

Adversity has the same effect on a man that severe training has on a pugilist—it reduces him to his fighting weight.   JOSH BILLINGS

It is a pleasant fact that you will know no man long, however low in the social scale, however poor, miserable, untemperate and worthless he may appear to be, a mere burden to society, but you will find at last that there is something he understands, and can do better than any other.
                                    HENRY DAVID THOREAU

Man is the only animal that blushes. Or needs to.
                                    MARK TWAIN

Let us be thankful for the fools. But for them the rest of us could not succeed.   MARK TWAIN

The hand that feeds us is in some danger of being bitten.   RALPH WALDO EMERSON

No great man ever complains of want of opportunity.   RALPH WALDO EMERSON

It takes your enemy and your friend, working together, to hurt you to the heart; the one to slander you, and the other to get the news to you.

MARK TWAIN

A man may have no bad habits and have worse.

MARK TWAIN

There are people who, if they ever reach heaven, will commence at once looking for their own set.

JOSH BILLINGS

Every hero becomes a bore at last.

RALPH WALDO EMERSON

No member of a crew is praised for the rugged individuality of his rowing.

RALPH WALDO EMERSON

The only sensible ends in literature are, first, the pleasurable toil of writing; second, the gratification of one's family and friends; and lastly, the solid cash.

NATHANIEL HAWTHORNE

Most men are like eggs: too full of themselves to hold anything else. JOSH BILLINGS

I'm opposed to millionaires, but it would be dangerous to offer me the position. MARK TWAIN

The art of art, the glory of expression, and the sunshine of the light of letters is simplicity. Nothing is better than simplicity. WALT WHITMAN

There are two times in a man's life when he should not speculate: when he can't afford it, and when he can. MARK TWAIN

There is a lust in man no charm can tame,
Of loudly publishing his neighbour's shame:
On eagles' wings immortal scandals fly,
While virtuous actions are but born and die.
ELLA LOUISA HARVEY

We often resolve to give up the care of the weather, but still we regard the clouds and the rain.
RALPH WALDO EMERSON

'If you would be a man speak what you think
today in words as hard as cannon balls, and
tomorrow speak what tomorrow thinks in hard
words again, though it contradict everything you
said today.' 'Ah, then!' exclaim the old ladies,
'you shall be sure to be misunderstood.' 'Misunderstood? It is a right fool's word. Is it so bad,
then, to be misunderstood? Pythagoras was misunderstood, and Socrates, and Jesus, and Luther,
and Copernicus, and Galileo, and Newton, and
every pure and wise spirit that ever took flesh. To
be great is to be misunderstood.'

RALPH WALDO EMERSON

That only profits which is profitable. Life alone
can impart life; and though we should burst, we
can only be valued as we make ourselves valuable.

RALPH WALDO EMERSON

Goodbye to flattery's fawning face;
To Grandeur, with his wise grimace;
To upstart Wealth's averted eye;
To supple Office, low and high;
To crowded halls, to court and street;
To frozen hearts and hastening feet;
To those who go, and those who come;
Goodbye, proud world! I'm going home.

RALPH WALDO EMERSON

Every ship is a romantic object, except that we sail in. Embark and the romance quits the vessel, and hangs on every other sail in the horizon.

RALPH WALDO EMERSON

The eyes of other people are the eyes that ruin us. If all but myself were blind, I should want neither fine clothes, fine houses, nor fine furniture.

BENJAMIN FRANKLIN

Die when I may, I want it said of me by those who knew me best, that I always plucked a thistle and planted a flower, where I thought a flower would grow.

ABRAHAM LINCOLN

I met a man in Oregon who hadn't any teeth—not a tooth in his head—yet that man could play the bass drum better than any man I ever met.

ARTEMUS WARD

I speak the password primeval; I give the sign of democracy. My God! I will accept nothing which all cannot have their counterpart of on the same terms.

WALT WHITMAN

Liberty, when it begins to take root, is a plant of rapid growth.   GEORGE WASHINGTON

★★★

You try to tell me anything about the newspaper business! Sir, I have been through it from Alpha to Omaha, and I tell you that the less a man knows, the bigger noise he makes, and the higher salary he commands.   MARK TWAIN

★★★

Science is a first class piece of furniture for a man's upper chamber, if he has commonsense on the ground floor.   OLIVER WENDELL HOLMES

★★★

With all respect for these ancient Israelites, I cannot overlook the fact that they were not always virtuous enough to withstand the seductions of the Golden Calf. Human nature has not changed much since then.   MARK TWAIN

★★★

The clergy, however, rarely hear any sermons except what they preach themselves. A dull preacher might be conceived, therefore, to lapse into a state of quasi-heathenism, simply for want of religious instruction.   OLIVER WENDELL HOLMES

Which I wish to remark—
And my language is plain,
That for ways that are dark,
And for tricks that are vain,
The heathen Chinee is peculiar—
Which the same I would rise to explain.

In his sleeves, which were long,
He had twenty-four packs—
Which was coming it strong,
Yet I state but the facts;
And we found in his nails, which were taper,
What is frequent in tapers—that's wax.

BRET HARTE

To brag a little—to show well—to crow gently, if
in luck—to pay up, to own up, and to shut up, if
beaten, are the virtues of a sporting man.

OLIVER WENDELL HOLMES

The greatest service we can do for another is to
help him to help himself. HENRY DAVID THOREAU

He who would enter into the realm of wisdom
must first divest himself of all intellectual pride.

HENRY DAVID THOREAU

A.W.W.—C.

Yet true to our course, though our shadow look
    dark,
  We'll trim our broad sail as before;
And stand by the rudder that governs the bark,
  Nor ask how we look from the shore.

                              OLIVER WENDELL HOLMES

★★★

Religion dying out? How can anything die out
before it is really born?   HENRY DAVID THOREAU

★★★

There's something ever egotistical in mountain-
tops and towers, and all other grand and lofty
things; look here, three peaks as proud as Lucifer.
The firm tower, that is Ahab; the volcano, that is
Ahab; the courageous, the undaunted, and
victorious fowl, that too is Ahab; all are Ahab.
From storm to storm! So be it, then. Born in
throes, 'tis fit that man should live in pains and die
in pangs. So be it then! Here's stout stuff for woe
to work on. So be it then!   HERMAN MELVILLE

★★★

Come all you rounders if you want to hear
A story all about a brave engineer.
Casey Jones was the rounder's name,
On a six-wheeler, boys he won his fame.

Casey Jones! mounted to the cabin.
Casey Jones! with his orders in his hand.
Casey Jones! mounted to the cabin
And took the farewell trip to the promised land.

He looked his watch and his watch was slow;
He looked at the river and the river was low;
He turned to the fireman and to him he said,
'We're going to get to Frisco or we'll all be dead.'

He pulled up within two miles of the place;
Number four stared him right in the face;
Turned to the fireman, 'Boy you better jump,
Here's two locomotives that are going to bump.'

ANONYMOUS

The highest condition of art is artlessness.

HENRY DAVID THOREAU

Confess your sins to the Lord and you will be
forgiven; confess them to man and you will be
laughed at.   JOSH BILLINGS

I cannot easily buy a blank book to write thoughts
in; they are commonly ruled for dollars and cents.

HENRY DAVID THOREAU

A great empire, like a great cake, is more easily diminished at the edges.   BENJAMIN FRANKLIN

There isn't a parallel of latitude but thinks it would have been the equator if it had had its rights.   MARK TWAIN

Fame is climbing a greasy pole for ten dollars, and ruining trousers worth fifteen dollars.
                                          JOSH BILLINGS

Most fools think they are only ignorant.
                                    BENJAMIN FRANKLIN

It is ill-manners to silence a fool, and cruelty to let him go on.   BENJAMIN FRANKLIN

In our country we have these three unspeakably precious things: freedom of speech, freedom of conscience, and the prudence never to practise either.   MARK TWAIN

To be intimate with a foolish friend is like going to bed with a razor. BENJAMIN FRANKLIN

Great geniuses have the shortest biographies; their cousins can tell you nothing about them.
RALPH WALDO EMERSON

Men have a singular desire to be good without being good for anything. HENRY DAVID THOREAU

What I value more than all things is good humor.
THOMAS JEFFERSON

The louder he talked of his honour the faster we counted the spoons. RALPH WALDO EMERSON

At present there is no distinction among the upper ten thousand of a city. NATHANIEL PARKER WILLIS

Towering genius disdains a beaten path. It seeks regions hitherto unexplored. ABRAHAM LINCOLN

All that we see or seem
Is but a dream within a dream.

EDGAR ALLAN POE

When a dog bites a man, that is not news; but when a man bites a dog, that is news.

CHARLES ANDERSON DANA

Why care for grammar as long as we are good?

ARTEMUS WARD

Let us be happy and live within our means even if we have to borrer the money to do it with.

ARTEMUS WARD

Labour to keep alive in your breast that little spark of celestial fire called conscience.

GEORGE WASHINGTON

***

The things that will destroy America are prosperity-at-any-price, peace-at-any-price, safety first instead of duty first, the love of soft living and the get-rich-quick theory of living.

THEODORE ROOSEVELT

The ship of democracy, which has weathered all storms, may sink through the mutiny of those on board.   GROVER CLEVELAND

An association of men who will not quarrel with one another is a thing which has never yet existed, from the greatest confederacy of nations down to a town meeting or a vestry.   THOMAS JEFFERSON

We must make the best of mankind as they are, since we cannot have them as we wish.
                          GEORGE WASHINGTON

In Flanders fields the poppies blow
Between the crosses, row on row,
    That mark our place, and in the sky
    The larks, still bravely singing, fly
Scarce heard amid the guns below.

We are the dead. Short days ago
We lived, felt dawn, saw sunset glow;
    Loved and were loved, and now we lie
        In Flanders fields.

Take up our quarrel with the foe:
To you, from failing hands we throw

The torch; be yours to hold it high.
If ye break faith with us who die,
We shall not sleep, though poppies grow
In Flanders fields.   JOHN McCRAE

★★★

Hence it happens that the whole interest of
history lies in the fortunes of the poor. Knowledge,
Virtue, Power, are the victories of man over his
necessities, his march to the dominion of the
world. Every man ought to have this opportunity
to conquer the world for himself. Only such people
interest us—Spartans, Romans, Saracens, English,
Americans—who have stood in the jaws of need,
and have by their own wit and might extricated
themselves and made man victorious.
                                        RALPH WALDO EMERSON

★★★

It is in vain, sir, to extenuate the matter. Gentlemen
may cry Peace, Peace—but there is no peace. The
war is already begun! The next gale that sweeps
from the north will bring to our ears the clash of
resounding arms! Our brethren are already in the
field! Why stand we here idle? What is it that
gentlemen wish? What would they have? Is life so
dear or peace so sweet as to be purchased at the
price of chains and slavery? Forbid it Almighty
God! I know not what course others may take, but
as for me, give me liberty, or give me death.
                                        PATRICK HENRY

The time is near at hand which must probably determine whether Americans are to be free men or slaves—the fate of unborn millions will now depend, under God, on the courage and conduct of the army. We have therefore to resolve to conquer or die. Let us therefore animate and encourage each other and show the whole world that a free man, contending for liberty on his own ground, is superior to any mercenary on earth.

GEORGE WASHINGTON

These are the times that try men's souls. The summer soldier and the sunshine patriot will, in this crisis, shrink from the service of his country. But he that stands it *now* deserves the love and thanks of man and woman. Tyranny, like hell, is not easily conquered yet we have this consolation with us, that the harder the conflict, the more glorious the triumph. What we obtain too cheap we esteem too lightly. 'Tis dearness only that gives everything its value. Heaven knows how to set a proper price upon its goods; and it would be strange indeed if so celestial an article as freedom should not be highly rated.

THOMAS PAINE

★★★

With malice toward none, with charity for all; with firmness in the right as God gives us to see the right, let us strive on to finish the work we are in; to bind up the nation's wounds, to care for him who

shall have borne the battle, and for his widow and
his orphan—to do all which may achieve and
cherish a just and lasting peace among ourselves,
and with all nations.   ABRAHAM LINCOLN

★★★

Joshua . . . never left any chance for newspaper
controversies about who won the battle.

MARK TWAIN

★★★

It is well known that fear has killed thousands of
victims; while, on the other hand, courage is a
great invigorator.   HENRY DAVID THOREAU

★★★

The race that shortens its weapons lengthens its
boundaries.   OLIVER WENDELL HOLMES

★★★

Mine eyes have seen the glory of the coming of
    the Lord;
He is trampling out the winepress where the
    grapes of wrath are stored.
He hath loosed the fateful lightning of His
    terrible swift sword;
His truth is marching on.

I have seen Him in the watchfires of a hundred
    circling camps;
They have builded Him an altar in the evening's
    dews and damps;
I can read His righteous sentence by the dim
    and flaring lamps.
    His day is marching on.   JULIA WARD HOWE

Fourscore and seven years ago our fathers brought
forth upon this continent a new nation, conceived
in liberty, and dedicated to the proposition that all
men are created equal. Now we are engaged in a
great civil war, testing whether that nation, or any
other nation so conceived and so dedicated, can
long endure. We are met on a great battlefield of
that war. We have come to dedicate a portion of
that field as a final resting place of those who here
gave their lives that that nation might live. It is
altogether fitting and proper that we should do
this. But in a larger sense, we cannot consecrate,
we cannot hallow this ground. The brave men,
living and dead, who struggled here, have con-
secrated it far above our poor power to add or
detract. The world will little note, nor long
remember, what we say here, but it can never
forget what they did here. It is for us, the living,
rather to be dedicated here to the unfinished work
they have thus far so nobly advanced. It is rather
for us to be here dedicated to the great task
remaining before us; that from these honoured
dead we take increased devotion to that cause for

which they here gave the last full measure of
devotion: that we here highly resolve that the dead
shall not have died in vain. That this nation under
God, shall have a new birth of freedom; and that
government of the people, by the people, and for
the people, shall not perish from the earth.

ABRAHAM LINCOLN

★★★

Hail Columbia! happy land!
Hail, ye heroes! heaven born band!
　Who fought and bled in Freedom's cause,
　Who fought and bled in Freedom's cause,
And when the storm of war was gone,
Enjoyed the peace your valor won.
　Let independence be your boast,
Ever mindful what it cost;
Ever grateful for the prize,
Let its altar reach the skies.
　Firm, united, let us be,
　　Rallying round our liberty;
　　As a band of brothers joined,
　　Peace and safety we shall find.

JOSEPH HOPKINSON

★★★

O say, can you see, by the dawn's early light,
What so proudly we hailed at the twilight's last
　　gleaming,
Whose broad stripes and bright stars, through
　　the clouds of the fight,

O'er the ramparts we watched were so gallantly
   streaming!
And the rocket's red glare, the bombs bursting
   in air,
Gave proof through the night that our flag was
   still there;
O! say, does that star spangled banner yet wave
O'er the land of the free, and the home of the
   brave?

O! thus be it ever; when freedom shall stand
Between their loved homes and the war's
   desolation!
Blest with victory and peace, may the heaven
   rescued land
Praise the power which hath made and preserved
   us a nation.
Then conquer we must, when our cause it is just,
And this be our motto: *In God is our trust.*
And the star spangled banner in triumph shall
   wave
O'er the land of the free, and the home of the
   brave.   FRANCIS SCOTT KEY

Ez fer war, I call it murder,
   There you hev it plain an' flat;
I don't want to go no furder
   Than my Testyment fer that;
God hez sed so plump an' fairly,
   It's ez long ez it is broad,

An' you've gut to git up airly
  Ef you want to take in God.

Wut's the use o' meetin'-goin'
  Every Sabbath wet or dry,
Ef it's right to go amowin'
  Feller-men like oats an' rye?
I dunna but wut it's pooty
  Trainin' round in bobtail coats,
But it's curus Christian dooty
  This 'ere cuttin' folks's throats.
JAMES RUSSELL LOWELL

★★★

Beat! beat! drums! blow! bugles! blow!
Make no parley, stop for no expostulation,
Mind not the timid, mind not the weeper or
    prayer,
Mind not the old man beseeching the young man,
Let not the child's voice be heard, nor the
    mother's entreaties,
Make even the trestles to shake the dead where
    they lie awaiting the hearses,
So strong you thump, O terrible drums, so loud
    you bugles blow.   WALT WHITMAN

★★★

All quiet along the Potomac tonight,
  No sound save the rush of the river,
While soft falls the dew on the face of the dead,
  The picket's off duty forever.   ETHEL LYNN BEERS

THE JUSTICE

They have a right to censure, that have a heart to
help. The rest is cruelty, not justice.

WILLIAM PENN

Make it a point to do something every day that you
don't want to do. This is the golden rule for
acquiring the habit of doing your duty without
pain. MARK TWAIN

When some men discharge an obligation you can
hear the report for miles around. MARK TWAIN

Nothing so needs reforming as other people's
habits. MARK TWAIN

No way of thinking or doing, however ancient, can
be trusted without proof. HENRY DAVID THOREAU

Don't never prophesy; for if you prophesy wrong,
nobody will forget it. And if you prophesy right,
nobody will remember it. JOSH BILLINGS

When the church is social worth,
When the state house is the hearth,
Then the perfect state is come;
The republican at home.

RALPH WALDO EMERSON

As a good chimney burns its smoke, so a philosopher converts the value of all his fortunes into his intellectual performances.

RALPH WALDO EMERSON

They are slaves who dare not be
In the right with two or three.

JAMES RUSSELL LOWELL

That 150 lawyers should do business together is not to be expected.   THOMAS JEFFERSON

Congress shall make no law respecting an establishment of religion, or prohibiting the free exercise thereof; or abridging the freedom of speech or of the press; or the right of the people peaceably to assemble and to petition the Government for a redress of grievances.   THE BILL OF RIGHTS

Give me your tired, your poor,
Your huddled masses yearning to breathe free;
The wretched refuse of your teeming shore.
Send these, the homeless, tempest tossed to me;
I lift the lamp beside the golden door.

EMMA LAZARUS

A man who is good enough to shed his blood for his country is good enough to be given a square meal afterwards. More than that no man is entitled to; and less than that no man shall have.

THEODORE ROOSEVELT

Judging merely by their general style, and without other evidence, one might easily suspect that self righteousness was their speciality.   MARK TWAIN

But I do mean to say that although bad laws, if they exist, should be repealed as soon as possible, still, while they continue in force, for the sake of example they should be religiously observed.

ABRAHAM LINCOLN

No man is good enough to govern another man without that other's consent.   ABRAHAM LINCOLN

There are steeple houses on every hand,
   And pulpits that bless and ban,
And the Lord will not grudge the single church
   That is set apart for man.

For in two commandments are all the law
   And the prophets under the sun,
And the first is last and the last is first,
   And the twain are verily one.

JOHN GREENLEAF WHITTIER

A countryman between two lawyers is like a fish between two cats.   BENJAMIN FRANKLIN

Faith keeps many doubts in her pay. If I could not doubt I should not believe.

HENRY DAVID THOREAU

A banker is a fellow who lends his umbrella when the sun is shining and wants it back the minute it begins to rain.   MARK TWAIN

I have lived in this world just long enough to look carefully the second time into things that I am most certain of the first time.   JOSH BILLINGS

No society can make a perpetual constitution, or
even a perpetual law.   THOMAS JEFFERSON

Swiftly arise and spread around me the peace
    and knowledge that pass all the argument
    of the earth,
And I know that the hand of God is the promise
    of my own,
And I know that the spirit of God is the brother
    of my own.   WALT WHITMAN

Whoever degrades another degrades me,
And what is done or said returns at last to me.
                    WALT WHITMAN

Lives of great men all remind us
    We can make our lives sublime;
And, departing, leave behind us
    Footprints in the sands of time.
            HENRY WADSWORTH LONGFELLOW

Where the population rise at once against the
never ending authority of elected people.
                    WALT WHITMAN

Learning is the art of knowing how to use common sense to advantage.   JOSH BILLINGS

★★★

To be a good critic demands more brains and judgment than most men possess.

JOSH BILLINGS

★★★

I hold these things to be self-evident: that all men are created equal; that they are endowed by their creator with *inherent* and inalienable rights; that among these are life, liberty and the pursuit of happiness.   THOMAS JEFFERSON

★★★

'I went right down to the jail and talked to that burglar. I told him how evil his life was. I told him how much happier he would be if he reformed. I talked to him for two hours.' 'Poor man', murmured OLIVER WENDELL HOLMES, 'poor man.'

★★★

And then when we fully realise the fact that selfishness is at the root of all error, sin and crime, and that ignorance is the basis of all selfishness; with what charity we come to look upon the acts of all.   HENRY DAVID THOREAU

When a man gets to talking about himself he seldom fails to be eloquent and often reaches the sublime.   JOSH BILLINGS

It is a maxim held by the courts that there is no wrong without its remedy.   ABRAHAM LINCOLN

There are some enterprises in which a careful disorderliness is the true method.

HERMAN MELVILLE

Oriental scenes look best in steel engravings. I cannot be imposed on any more by that picture of the Queen of Sheba visiting Solomon. I shall say to myself, 'Your Majesty looks fine, but your feet are not clean, and you smell like a camel.'

MARK TWAIN

Fish and visitors smell in three days.

BENJAMIN FRANKLIN

The execution of the laws is more important than the making of them.   THOMAS JEFFERSON

Duties are not performed for duty's sake, but because their neglect would make the man uncomfortable. A man performs but one duty, the duty of contenting his spirit, the duty of making himself agreeable to himself.   MARK TWAIN

Laws are enacted for the benefit of the whole people, and cannot and must not be construed as permitting discrimination against some of the people. I am President of all the people of the United States, without regard to creed, color, birthplace, occupation, or social condition.

THOMAS JEFFERSON

What is the use of being elected or re-elected unless you stand for something?

GROVER CLEVELAND

Zoroaster said, 'When in doubt abstain', but this does not always apply. At cards, when in doubt, take the trick.   JOSH BILLINGS

There are few persons who have not, at some period in their lives, amused themselves by retracing the steps by which a particular conclusion of their own minds has been attained. The occupation is often full of interest; and he who attempts it for the first time is astonished by the apparently illimitable distance between the starting point and the goal.   EDGAR ALLAN POE

The memorable thought, the happy expression, the adorable deed are only partly ours.

HENRY DAVID THOREAU

I have made it a rule never to smoke more than one cigar at a time.   MARK TWAIN

Part of the secret of success in life is to eat what you like and let the food fight it out inside.

MARK TWAIN

Remember the poor; it costs nothing.

JOSH BILLINGS

Few of us can stand prosperity. Another man's I mean.   MARK TWAIN

Why, bless my soul, if all the cities in the world
were reduced to ashes, you'd have a new set of
millionaires in a couple of years or so; out of the
trade in potash.   OLIVER WENDELL HOLMES

Men are conservatives when they are least
vigorous, or when they are most luxurious. They
are conservatives after dinner.
                          RALPH WALDO EMERSON

Plain Tom and Dick would pass as current now,
As ever since, 'Your servant, Sir!' and bow.
Deep-skirted doublets, puritanic capes,
Which now would render men like upright apes,
Were comelier wear, our wiser fathers thought,
Than the cast fashions from all Europe brought.
'Twas in those days an honest grace would hold
Till an hot pudding grew at heart a cold,
And men had better stomachs at religion,
Than I to capon, turkey cock, or pigeon;
When honest sisters met to pray, not prate,
About their own and not their neighbour's state.
                          BENJAMIN TOMPSON

If fresh meat be wanting to fill up our dish,
We have carrots and turnips as much as we wish:
And if there's a mind for a delicate dish

We repair to the clam-banks, and there we
    catch fish.
Instead of pottage and puddings and custards
    and pies,
Our pumpkins and parsnips are common supplies;
We have pumpkins at morning and pumpkins
    at noon,
If it was not for pumpkins we should be undone!
But bring both a quiet and contented mind,
And all needful blessings you surely will find.

                      BENJAMIN TOMPSON

The demon of intemperance ever seems to have
delighted in sucking the blood of genius and
generosity.   ABRAHAM LINCOLN

I shall never want another Turkish lunch . . . the
fellow took a mass of sausage meat and coated it
round a wire, and laid it on a charcoal fire to cook.
When it was done he laid it aside, and a dog
walked sadly in and nipped it. He smelt it first and
probably recognized the remains of an old friend.

                        MARK TWAIN

                ★★★

I knew then what I had sometimes known before—
that it is worth while to get tired out, because one
so enjoys resting afterwards.   MARK TWAIN

Indeed I believe, if we take habitual drunkards as a class, their heads and their hearts will bear an advantageous comparison with those of any other class.   ABRAHAM LINCOLN

A man may own and live in a palace, but the palace for him may be a poorhouse still.
                                    HENRY DAVID THOREAU

It usually takes more than three weeks to prepare a good impromptu speech.   MARK TWAIN

Temperate temperance is best. Intemperate temperance injures the cause of temperance. MARK TWAIN

All the thoughts of a turtle are turtle.
                                    RALPH WALDO EMERSON

In general, mankind, since the improvement of cookery, eats twice as much as nature requires.
                                    BENJAMIN FRANKLIN

It has always been my rule never to smoke while asleep, and never to refrain when awake.

MARK TWAIN

Not for delectation sweet,
Not the cushion and the slipper, not the
    peaceful and the studious,
Not the riches, safe and palling, not for us the
    tame enjoyment,
        Pioneers! O pioneers!

Do the feasters gluttonous feast?
Do the corpulent sleepers sleep? have they
    lock'd and bolted doors?
Still be ours the diet hard, and the blanket on
    the ground,
        Pioneers! O pioneers!   WALT WHITMAN

A solid man of Boston,
A comfortable man with dividends
And the first salmon and the first green peas.

HENRY WADSWORTH LONGFELLOW

On the continent you can't get a rare beef steak, everything is as overdone as a martyr.

MARK TWAIN

He had much experience of physicians, and said
'the only way to keep your health is to eat what
you don't want, drink what you don't like, and do
what you druther not.'   MARK TWAIN

Hunger is the handmaid of genius.   MARK TWAIN

Three good meals a day is bad living.
                                    BENJAMIN FRANKLIN

The lack of money is the root of all evil.
                                    MARK TWAIN

I can't sing. As a singist I am not a success. I am
saddest when I sing. So are those who hear me.
They are sadder even than I am.
                                    ARTEMUS WARD

E'en in thy native regions how I blush
To hear the Pennsylvanians call thee *Mush*!
On Hudson's banks, where men of Belgic spawn
Insult and eat thee by the name *Suppawn*.

All spurious appellations, void of truth;
I've better known thee from my earliest youth:
The name is *Hasty-Pudding*! Thus my sire
Was wont to greet thee fuming from the fire;
And while he argued in thy just defense
With logic clear, he thus explained the sense:
In haste the boiling cauldron, o'er the blaze,
Receives and cooks the ready powdered maize;
In haste 'tis served, and then in equal haste
With cooling milk we make the sweet repast.
JOEL BARLOW

Let us not underrate the value of a fact—it will
one day flower into a truth.
HENRY DAVID THOREAU

Advertisements contain the only truths to be
relied on in a newspaper.   THOMAS JEFFERSON

Advice is a drug on the market; the supply always
exceeds the demand.   JOSH BILLINGS

★★★

Almost any fool can prove that the Bible ain't so—
it takes a wise man to believe it.   JOSH BILLINGS

City life: millions of people being lonely together.
                              HENRY DAVID THOREAU

Some circumstantial evidence is very strong, as when you find a trout in the milk.
                              HENRY DAVID THOREAU

It is only by forgetting yourself that you draw near to God.   HENRY DAVID THOREAU

Men talk about Bible miracles because there is no miracle in their own lives.
                              HENRY DAVID THOREAU

We often feel sad in the presence of music without words: and often more than that in the presence of music without music.   MARK TWAIN

Let us reflect that the highest path is pointed out by the pure ideal of those who look up to us, and who, if we tread less loftily, may never look so high again.   NATHANIEL HAWTHORNE

I don't know a single product that enters this
country untaxed, except the answer to prayer.

MARK TWAIN

Visit your aunt, but not every day; and call at your
brother's; but not every night.

BENJAMIN FRANKLIN

Creditors have better memories than debtors.

BENJAMIN FRANKLIN

If you would keep a secret from an enemy, tell it
not to a friend.   BENJAMIN FRANKLIN

If you would know the value of money, go and try
to borrow some.   BENJAMIN FRANKLIN

★★★

No man ever saw a gray hair on the head or beard
of any truth.   NATHANIEL HAWTHORNE

★★★

If you pick up a starving dog and make him
A.W.W.—D

prosperous he will not bite you. This is the principal difference between a dog and a man.

MARK TWAIN

You can fool all the people some of the time, and some of the people all the time, but you cannot fool all the people all the time.

Attributed both to ABRAHAM LINCOLN
and to PHINEAS T. BARNUM

The word Palestine always brought to my mind a vague suggestion of a country as large as the United States. I suppose it was because I could not conceive of a small country having so large a history.

MARK TWAIN

Shakespeare is always present when one reads his book; Macaulay is present when we follow the march of his stately sentences; but the Old Testament writers are hidden from view.

MARK TWAIN

One must stand upon his head to get the best effect in a fine sunset.

MARK TWAIN

Do not mistake that the ballot is stronger than the bullet. ABRAHAM LINCOLN

You need never think you can turn over any old falsehood without a terrible squirming and scattering of the horrid little population that dwells under it. OLIVER WENDELL HOLMES

The parson was working his Sunday text—
Had got to fifthly, and stopped perplexed,
At what the—Moses—was coming next.
OLIVER WENDELL HOLMES

End of the wonderful one-hoss-shay,
Logic is logic. That's all I say.
OLIVER WENDELL HOLMES

A nail will pick a lock that defies hatchet and hammer. OLIVER WENDELL HOLMES

The great fundamental principles of all religions are the same. HENRY DAVID THOREAU

Grant us Thy truth to make us free,
  And kindling hearts that burn for Thee.
Till all Thy living altars claim
  One Holy light, one heavenly flame.

OLIVER WENDELL HOLMES

★★★

Almost any man knows how to earn money, but
not one in a million knows how to spend it.

HENRY DAVID THOREAU

★★★

As if we could kill time without injuring eternity.

HENRY DAVID THOREAU

★★★

Never put off to tomorrow what you can do the
day after tomorrow just as well.   MARK TWAIN

★★★

Half a truth is often a great lie.

BENJAMIN FRANKLIN

★★★

Men wish to be saved from the mischiefs of their
virtues, but not from their vices.

RALPH WALDO EMERSON

He is not well-bred that cannot bear ill-breeding in others.   BENJAMIN FRANKLIN

Laughing is the sensation of feeling good all over, and showing it principally in one spot.

JOSH BILLINGS

Every individual has a place to fill in the world, and is important in some respect, whether he chooses to be so or not.   NATHANIEL HAWTHORNE

A person seldom falls sick, but the bystanders are animated with a faint hope that he will die.

RALPH WALDO EMERSON

The autocrat of Russia possesses more power than any man in the earth, but he cannot stop a sneeze.

MARK TWAIN

When we remember that we all are mad, the mysteries disappear and life stands explained.

MARK TWAIN

Be virtuous and you will be eccentric.

MARK TWAIN

It takes a man to make a room silent.

HENRY DAVID THOREAU

There ain't no way to find out why a snorer can't hear himself snore.   MARK TWAIN

Whenever you find that you are on the side of the majority, it is time to reform.   MARK TWAIN

Good manners are made up of petty sacrifices.

RALPH WALDO EMERSON

Everyone is a moon, and has a dark side which he never shows to anybody.   MARK TWAIN

Let us not be too particular; it is better to have old second-hand diamonds than none at all.

MARK TWAIN

These are two kinds of fools: those who can't change their minds and those who won't.

JOSH BILLINGS

Be careless in your dress if you must, but keep a tidy soul. MARK TWAIN

Learning sleeps and snores in libraries but wisdom is everywhere, wide awake, on tip toes.

JOSH BILLINGS

Let us be grateful to Adam our benefactor. He cut us out of the *blessing* of idleness, and won for us the *curse* of labour. MARK TWAIN

You can straighten a worm, but the crook is in him and only waiting. MARK TWAIN

Every reform is only a mask under cover of which a more terrible reform, which does not yet name itself, advances. RALPH WALDO EMERSON

Every reform was once a private opinion.
RALPH WALDO EMERSON

The generation which commences a revolution, rarely completes it.   THOMAS JEFFERSON

The rich should remember that when they reach heaven they will find Lazarus there, and have to be polite to him.   JOSH BILLINGS

No man is rich who wants more than he has got.
JOSH BILLINGS

Different sects, like different clocks, may be all near the matter, though they don't quite agree.
JOSH BILLINGS

Few sinners are saved after the first twenty minutes of a sermon.   MARK TWAIN

THE LEAN
AND SLIPPER'D
PANTALOON

The woods are the true temple for there the thoughts are free to mount higher even than the clouds.
                                    FENIMORE COOPER

'What do you see when you get there?'
'Creation: all creation, lad. How should a man who has lived in towns and schools know anything about the wonders of the woods?'
                                    FENIMORE COOPER

I came into this world, not chiefly to make this a good place to live in, but to live in it, be it good or bad. A man has not everything to do, but something; and because he cannot do everything it is not necessary that he should do something wrong.
                                    HENRY DAVID THOREAU

I claim not to have controlled events, but confess plainly that events have controlled me.
                                    ABRAHAM LINCOLN

I admire the serene assurance of those who have religious faith. It is wonderful to observe the calm confidence of a Christian with four aces.
                                    MARK TWAIN

Faith is the soul riding at anchor.   JOSH BILLINGS

Blest is the nation whose silent course of happiness furnishes nothing for history to say. This is what I ambition for my country.   THOMAS JEFFERSON

The youth gets together materials for a bridge to the moon, and at length the middle-aged man decides to make a wood-shed with them.

HENRY DAVID THOREAU

Solitude is a good place to visit but a poor place to stay.   JOSH BILLINGS

The nation behaves well if it treats the natural resources as assets which it must turn over to the next generation increased, and not impaired in value.   THEODORE ROOSEVELT

But they sailed serenely away and paid no further heed to pilgrims who had dreamed all their lives of some day skimming over the sacred waters of Galilee, and listening to its hallowed story in the

whisperings of its waves, and had journeyed countless leagues to do it—and then concluded that the fare was too high.   MARK TWAIN

Memory, imagination, old sentiments and associations, are more readily reached through the sense of smell than by almost any other channel.

OLIVER WENDELL HOLMES

Men, like peaches and pears, grow sweet a little while before they begin to decay.

OLIVER WENDELL HOLMES

Would you remain always young, and would you carry all the joyousness and buoyancy of youth into your maturer years? Then have care concerning one thing—how you live in the thought world.

HENRY DAVID THOREAU

Men are kept in continual ill health by the abnormal thought and attention they give them. Give the body the nourishment, the exercise, the fresh air and the sunlight it requires, keep it clean, and then think about it as little as possible.

HENRY DAVID THOREAU

Wiser far than human seer,
Yellow breeched philosopher!
Seeing only what is fair,
Sipping only what is sweet,
Thou dost mock at fate and care,
Leave the chaff and take the wheat.
When the fierce northwestern blast
Cools sea and land so far and fast,
Thou already slumberest deep;
Woe and want thou canst outsleep;
Want and woe, which torture us,
Thy sleep makes ridiculous.

RALPH WALDO EMERSON

The horseman serves the horse,
The neatherd serves the neat,
The merchant serves the purse,
The eater serves his meat;
'Tis the day of the chattel,
Web to weave and corn to grind;
Things are in the saddle,
And ride mankind.   RALPH WALDO EMERSON

A year has gone as the tortoise goes
    Heavy and slow;
And the same rose blooms and the same sun
    glows,
    And the same brook sings of a year ago.

JOHN GREENLEAF WHITTIER

God pity them both! and pity us all,
Who vainly the dreams of youth recall.

For all sad words of tongue or pen,
The saddest are these: 'It might have been!'

JOHN GREENLEAF WHITTIER

I find friendship to be like wine, raw when new,
ripened with age, the true old man's milk and
restorative cordial.

THOMAS JEFFERSON

I saw him once before,
As he passed by the door,
    And again
The pavement stones resound,
As he totters o'er the ground
    With his cane.

They say that in his prime,
Ere the pruning hook of Time
    Cut him down,
Not a better man was found
By the Crier on his round
    Through the town.

But now he walks the streets,
And he looks at all he meets
    Sad and wan,
And he shakes his feeble head,

That it seems as if he said,
  'They are gone.'

But now his nose is thin,
And it rests upon his chin
  Like a staff,
And a crook is in his back,
And a melancholy crack
  In his laugh.

And if I should live to be
The last leaf upon the tree
  In the spring,
Let them smile, as I do now
At the old forsaken bough
  Where I cling.   OLIVER WENDELL HOLMES

★★★

O Spirit of that early day,
  So pure and strong and true,
Be with us in the narrow way
  Our faithful fathers knew.
Give strength the evil to forsake,
  The cross of truth to bear,
And love the reverent fear to make
  Our daily lives a prayer.
                      JOHN GREENLEAF WHITTIER

★★★

But still my human hands are weak
  To hold your iron creeds:

Against the words ye bid me speak
  My heart within me pleads.

Who fathoms the Eternal Thought?
  Who talks of scheme and plan?
The Lord is God! He heedeth not
  The poor device of man.

Ye see the curse which overbroods
  A world of pain and loss;
I hear our Lord's beatitudes
  And prayer upon the cross.

Yet in the maddening maze of things
  And tossed by storm and flood,
To one fixed trust my spirit clings;
  I know that God is good!

JOHN GREENLEAF WHITTIER

Sweeter than hope's sweet lute
  Singing of joys to be,
When Pain's harsh voice is mute,
  Is the Soul's sweet song to me.

THOMAS HOLLEY CHIVERS

They seemed
Like old companions in adversity.

HENRY DAVID THOREAU

The heights by great men reached and kept
   Were not attained by sudden flight,
But they while their companions slept
   Were toiling upward in the night.
HENRY WADSWORTH LONGFELLOW

He who has a thousand friends has
   Not a friend to spare;
And he who has one enemy will meet
   Him everywhere.   RALPH WALDO EMERSON

Such is the human race. Often it does seem such a
pity that Noah and his party didn't miss the boat.
MARK TWAIN

Life is a great bundle of little things.
OLIVER WENDELL HOLMES

We live but a fraction of our life.
HENRY DAVID THOREAU

Civilisation is a limitless multiplication of un-
necessary necessaries.   MARK TWAIN

SECOND CHILDISHNESS

All round de little farm I wandered
  When I was young,
Den many happy days I squandered,
  Many de songs I sung.
When I was playing wid my brother,
  Happy was I;
Oh, take me to my kind old mudder!
  Dere let me live and die.   STEPHEN FOSTER

When de autumn leaves were falling,
  When de days were cold,
'Twas hard to hear old massa calling,
  Cayse he was so weak and old.
Now de orange trees am blooming
  On de sandy shore,
Now de summer days am coming,
  Massa never calls no more.   STEPHEN FOSTER

An old man in a house is a good sign.
                        BENJAMIN FRANKLIN

***

Were it offered to my choice, I should have no
objection to a repetition of the same life from its
beginning, only asking the advantages authors
have in a second edition, to correct some of the
faults of the first.   BENJAMIN FRANKLIN

I have never known a person to live to 110 or more,
and then die, and be remarkable for anything else.
JOSH BILLINGS

Let the soul be assured that somewhere in the
universe it should rejoin its friend, and it would be
content and cheerful alone for a thousand years.
RALPH WALDO EMERSON

Each lonely place shall him restore,
    For him the tear be duly shed;
Beloved till life can charm no more;
    And mourned till pity's self be dead.
WASHINGTON IRVING

Earth gets its price for what Earth gives us;
    The beggar is taxed for a corner to die in,
The priest hath his fee who comes and shrives us;
    We bargain for the graves we lie in;
At the devil's booth all things are sold,
Each ounce of dross costs its ounce of gold;
    For a cap and bells our lives we pay,
Bubbles we buy for a whole soul's tasking.
    'Tis heaven alone that is given away,
'Tis only God may be had for the asking.
JAMES RUSSELL LOWELL

Q. Who is this picture of on the wall? Isn't it a
brother of yours?

A. Ah, yes, yes, yes! Now you remind me of it;
that was a brother of mine. That's William—
Bill we called him. Poor old Bill!

Q. Why? Is he dead, then?

A. Ah well, I suppose so. We never could tell.
There was a great mystery about it.

Q. That is sad, very sad. He disappeared then?

A. Well, yes, in a sort of general way. We buried
him.

Q. Buried him! Buried him without knowing
whether he was dead or not?

A. Oh no! Not that. He was dead enough.

Q. Well, I confess that I can't understand this. If
you buried him, and you knew he was dead. . . .

A. Oh no! We only thought he was.

Q. Oh I see! He came to life again?

A. I bet he didn't.

Q. Well, I never heard anything like this. *Somebody*
was dead. *Somebody* was buried. Now where was
the mystery?

A. Ah, that's just it. That's it exactly. You see, we
were twins, defunct and I, and we got mixed
in the bathtub when we were only two weeks
old, and one of us was drowned. But we don't
know which. Some think it was Bill, some think
it was me.

Q. Well, that is remarkable! What do *you* think?

A. Goodness knows! I would give whole worlds to
know. This solemn, this awful mystery, has cast
a gloom over my whole life. But I will tell you
a secret now which I have never revealed to

any creature before. One of us had a peculiar
mark—a large mole on the back of his left hand.
That was me. *That was the one who was drowned.*

MARK TWAIN

★★★

The healing of His seamless dress
  Is by our beds of pain;
We touch Him in life's throng and press,
  And we are whole again.

Our Friend, our Brother, and our Lord,
  What may Thy service be?
Nor name, nor form, nor ritual word,
  But simply following Thee.

We faintly hear, we dimly see,
  In differing phrase we pray;
But dim or clear, we own in Thee
  The Light, the Truth, the Way.

JOHN GREENLEAF WHITTIER

★★★

And yet, when all is thought and said,
The heart still over-rules the head;
Still what we hope we must believe,
And what is given us receive.

Must still believe, for still we hope
That in a world of larger scope,

What here is faithfully begun
Will be completed, not undone.
                    ARTHUR HUGH CLOUGH

★★★

Say not the struggle naught availeth,
    The labour and the wounds are vain,
The enemy faints not nor faileth,
    And as things have been, they remain.

If hopes were dupes, fears may be liars;
    It may be in yon smoke concealed,
Your comrades chase e'en now the fliers,
    And, but for you, possess the field.

For while the tired waves, vainly breaking,
    Seem here no painful inch to gain,
Far back, through creeks and inlets making,
    Comes silent, flooding in, the main.

And not by eastern windows only,
    When daylight comes, comes in the light;
In front the sun climbs slow, how slowly.
    But westward look, the land is bright.
                    ARTHUR HUGH CLOUGH

★★★

Daughters of time, the hypocritic Days,
Muffled and dumb like barefoot dervishes,
And marching single in an endless file
Bring diadems and fagots in their hands.

To each they offer gifts after his will,
Bread, kingdoms, stars, and sky that holds them
    all.
I in my pleached garden watched the pomp,
Forgot my morning wishes, hastily
Took a few herbs and apples, and the Day
Turned, and departed silent. I, too late,
Under that solemn fillet saw the scorn.

RALPH WALDO EMERSON

I am the owner of the sphere,
Of the seven stars and the solar year,
Of Caesar's hand and Plato's brain,
Of Lord Christ's heart, and Shakespeare's strain.

RALPH WALDO EMERSON

Where lies the land to which the ship would go?
Far, far ahead, is all her seamen know.
And where the land she travels from? Away,
Far, far behind, is all that they can say.

ARTHUR HUGH CLOUGH

★★★

There is a ripeness of time for death . . . when it is
reasonable we should drop off, and make room for
another growth. When we have lived our generation out, we should not wish to encroach on
another.   THOMAS JEFFERSON

O Time! the fatal wrack of mortal things,
  That draws oblivion's curtains over kings,
Their sumptuous monuments, men know them
    not,
  Their names without a record are forgot;
Their parts, their ports, their pomp's all laid i'
    the dust,
Nor wit nor gold, nor buildings 'scape Time's
    rust:
But he whose name is grav'd in the white stone
Shall last and shine when all of these are gone.

ANNE BRADSTREET

As the bird trims her to the gale,
I trim myself to the storm of time;
I man the rudder, reef the sail,
Obey the voice at even obeyed at prime:
'Lowly faithful, banish fear,
Right onward drive unharmed;
The port, well worth the cruise, is near,
And every wave is charmed.'

RALPH WALDO EMERSON

O Holy Night! from thee I learn to bear
  What man has borne before!
Thou layest thy finger on the lips of Care
  And they complain no more.

HENRY WADSWORTH LONGFELLOW

He who from zone to zone,
Guides through the boundless sky thy certain
    flight,
In the long way that I must tread alone,
  Will lead my steps aright.

WILLIAM CULLEN BRYANT

★★★

So live, that, when thy summons comes to join
The innumerable caravan, that moves
To that mysterious realm, where each shall take
His chamber in the silent halls of death,
Thou go not, like the quarry slave, at night,
Scourged to his dungeon, but, sustained and
    soothed
By an unfaltering trust, approach thy grave,
Like one that draws the drapery of his couch
About him, and lies down to pleasant dreams.

WILLIAM CULLEN BRYANT

★★★

And he gathers the prayers as he stands,
And they change into flowers in his hands,
  Into garlands of purple and red;
And beneath the great arch of the portal,
Through the streets of the City Immortal
  Is wafted the fragrance they shed.

And the legend I feel, is a part
Of the hunger and thirst of the heart,
  The frenzy and fire of the brain,

That grasps at the fruitage forbidden,
The golden pomegranates of Eden,
   To quiet its fever and pain.
HENRY WADSWORTH LONGFELLOW

In the long sleepless watches of the night,
   A gentle face, the face of one long dead,
   Looks at me from the wall, where round its
      head
   The night-lamp casts a halo of pale light.
Here in this room she died; and soul more white
   Never through martyrdom of fire was led
   To its repose; nor can in books be read
   The legend of a life more benedight.
There is a mountain in the distant West
   That, sun-defying, in its deep ravines
   Displays a cross of snow upon its side.
Such is the cross I wear upon my breast
These eighteen years, through all the changing
      scenes
And seasons, changeless since the day she died.
HENRY WADSWORTH LONGFELLOW

As a fond mother, when the day is o'er,
   Leads by the hand her little child to bed,
   Half willing, half reluctant to be led,
   And leave his broken playthings on the floor,
Still gazing at them through the open door,
   Nor wholly reassured and comforted

By promises of others in their stead,
  Which, though more splendid, may not please
    him more;
So Nature deals with us, and takes away
  Our playthings one by one, and by the hand
  Leads us to rest so gently, that we go
Scarce knowing if we wish to go or stay,
  Being too full of sleep to understand
  How far the unknown transcends the what we
    know.

HENRY WADSWORTH LONGFELLOW

★★★

The Pilgrim Fathers, where are they?
  The waves that brought them o'er
Still roll in the bay, and throw their spray
  As they break along the shore:
Still roll in the bay, as they rolled that day
  When the *Mayflower* moor'd below,
When the sea around was black with storms,
  And white the shore with snow.

The Pilgrim spirit has not fled;
  It walks the noon's broad light;
And it watches the bed of the glorious dead,
  With their holy stars, by night.
It watches the bed of the brave who have bled,
  And shall guard this ice-bound shore,
Till the waves of the bay, where the *Mayflower* lay,
  Shall foam and freeze no more.

JOHN PIERPONT

Mid pleasures and palaces though we may roam,
Be it ever so humble, there's no place like home;
A charm from the sky seems to hallow us there,
Which, seek through the world, is ne'er met with
    elsewhere.
Home, Home, sweet Home!
There's no place like Home! There's no place
    like Home!

An exile from home; splendour dazzles in vain;
O give me my lowly thatched cottage again!
The birds singing gaily, that came at my call,
Give me them, and the peace of mind dearer
    than all!
Home, Home, sweet Home!
There's no place like Home! there's no place
    like Home!

JOHN HOWARD PAYNE

Delight is to him a far, far upward, and inward
delight, who against the proud gods and com-
modores of this earth, ever stands forth his own
inexorable self. Delight is to him whose strong
arms yet support him, when the ship of this base,
treacherous world has gone down beneath him.
Delight is to him who gives no quarter in the
truth, and kills, burns and destroys all sin though
he pluck it out from under the robes of Senators
and Judges. Delight, top gallant delight is to him,
who acknowledges no law or lord, but the Lord his

God, and is only a patriot to heaven. Delight is to him, whom all the waves of the billows of the seas of the boisterous mob can never shake from this sure Keel of the Ages. And eternal delight and deliciousness will be his, who, coming to lay him down, can say with his final breath 'O Father! chiefly known to me by Thy rod, mortal or immortal, here I die. I have striven to be Thine, more than to be this world's, or mine own. Yet this is nothing; I leave Eternity to Thee; for what is man that he should live out the lifetime of his God?'

HERMAN MELVILLE

★★★

I hear and behold God in every object, yet
    understand God not in the least,
Nor do I understand who there can be more
    wonderful than myself.
Why should I wish to see God better than this
    day?
I see something of God each hour of the twenty
    four, and each moment then,
In the face of men and women I see God, and
    in my own face in the glass,
I find letters from God dropped in the street,
    and every one is signed by God's name,
And I leave them where they are, for I know
    that whereso'er I go,
Others will punctually come for ever and ever.

WALT WHITMAN

When lilacs last in the doorway bloom'd,
And the great star early droop'd in the western
    sky in the night,
I mourn'd and yet shall mourn with ever-
    returning spring.

Ever-returning spring, trinity sure to me you
    bring,
Lilac blooming perennial and drooping star in
    the west,
And thought of him I love.   WALT WHITMAN

Behold a woman!
She looks out from her quaker cap, her face is
    clearer and more beautiful than the sky.
She sits in an armchair under the shaded porch
    of the farmhouse,
The sun just shines on her old white head.
Her ample gown is of cream-hued linen,
Her grandsons raised the flax and her grand-
    daughters spun it with the distaff and the
    wheel.
The melodious character of the earth,
The finish beyond which philosophy cannot go
    and does not wish to go,
The justified mother of men.   WALT WHITMAN

O, by an' by, by an' by,
I'm gwineter lay down my heavy load.

A.W.W.—E

I know my robe's gwineter fit me well
I tried it on at de gates of Hell.

O, by an' by, by an' by,
I'm gwineter lay down my heavy load.

O, Hell's a deep and dark despair,
O stop, po' sinner, an' don' go there.

O, one of dose mornin's bright an' fair,
(I'm gwineter lay down my heavy load.)
I'll put on my wings an' cleave de air.
(I'm gwineter lay down my heavy load.)

SPIRITUAL

★★★

'O bury me not on the lone prairie!'
These words came low and mournfully,
From the pallid lips of a youth who lay
On his dying bed at the close of day.

'I've always hoped to be laid when I died,
In the old churchyard 'neath the green hillside,
Where friends might meet and weep over me;
O, bury me not on the lone prairie!'

'O bury me not'—and his voice failed there,
But we heeded not to his dying prayer.
In a narrow grave just six by three
We buried him there on the lone prairie.

COWBOY BALLAD

Live I, so live I,
  To my Lord heartily,
  To my Prince faithfully,
  To my neighbour honestly,
Die I, so die I. HENRY WADSWORTH LONGFELLOW

No Cross, no Crown. WILLIAM PENN

O my brave soul!
O farther, farther sail!
O daring joy, but safe; are they not all the seas
  of God?
O farther, farther, farther sail! WALT WHITMAN

Never to have suffered would have been never to
have been blessed. EDGAR ALLAN POE

BIOGRAPHICAL NOTES

BIOGRAPHICAL NOTES

Adams, John (1735–1826), President of the United States (1797–1801). He was a signatory to the Declaration of Independence.

Barlow, Joel (1754–1812), teacher, poet and diplomat. His best known works are *The Vision of Columbus* (1787) and *Advice to the Privileged Orders* (1792). He was influenced by Thomas Paine (*q.v.*).

Barnum, Phineas Taylor (1810–91), showman. He first gained fame by exhibiting freaks in his American Museum. In 1871 he opened his circus which he called 'The Greatest Show on Earth'.

Beers, Ethel Lynn, pseudonym of Ethelinda Eliot Beers (1827–79), poet and short-story writer.

Billings, Josh, pseudonym of Henry Wheeler Shaw (1818–85), lecturer and writer of humorous essays. He wrote in an exaggerated New England and New York rural dialect and was considerably influenced by Artemus Ward (*q.v.*). Among his works are *Sayings* (1865, 1866) and *Josh Billings on Ice and Other Things* (1868).

Bradstreet, Anne (*c.* 1612–72), poet of the Massachusetts Bay Colony, born in England. An edition of her poems was published in 1650 under the title *The Tenth Muse Lately Sprung Up in America*.

Brainard, John Gardiner Calkins (1796–1828), newspaperman.

Bryant, William Cullen (1794–1878), poet, critic and editor. His poems were first published in 1817. He later became editor of the New York *Evening Post*. His best known works include *The Embargo* (1808), *Thanatopsis* (1317) and *The Flood of Years* (1876).

Chivers, Thomas Holley (1809–58), poet and physician. His volumes of verse include *The Lost Pleiad and Other Poems* (1845) and *Virginia* (1853).

Cleveland, Stephen Grover (1837–1908), twice President of the United States (1885–89; 1893–97). Under his administration the Sherman Silver Purchase Act was repealed, ending the drain on U.S. gold reserves. In 1894 he sent troops into Illinois to combat interference with the movement of mail by strikers.

Clough, Arthur Hugh (1819–61), English poet. He enjoyed a close friendship with Emerson (*q.v.*) and in 1852 lectured at Harvard. His best known work is the short lyric 'Say not the struggle naught availeth'.

Cooper, James Fenimore (1789–1851), novelist. Author of *The Pioneers* (1823) and *The Pilot* (in which the character of Natty Bumppo first appears), he was a prolific writer and an open critic of what he saw as the decline of American democracy. Probably his best known work is *The Last of the Mohicans* (1826).

Crockett, Davy (1786–1836), frontiersman and folk hero. Elected to Congress for three terms (1827–31; 1833–35), he was known as 'the Coonskin Congressman'. *A Narrative of the Life of David Crockett* (1834) is attributed to him.

Dana, Charles Anderson (1819–97), journalist. He built the New York *Sun* into one of the leading newspapers in the United States, employing some of the best writers of the day.

Dana, Richard Henry Jr. (1815–82), lawyer and writer. He worked as a seaman in an effort to improve his health. From his experiences he wrote *Two Years Before the Mast* (1840) which drew attention to the plight of the ordinary sailor.

Drake, Joseph Rodman (1795–1820), poet and satirist. His best known work is *The Culprit Fay* (published 1835).

Emerson, Ralph Waldo (1803–82), poet, essayist and philosopher. He became a Unitarian pastor but three years later found he could not accept the church's doctrine. He made several trips to Europe, and in Concord, Mass., formed a group with, among others, Henry David Thoreau (*q.v.*) and Margaret Fuller. This group was the centre of American transcendentalism. He recorded his philosophical thoughts in *Nature* (1836).

Emmet, Daniel Decatur (1815–1904), songwriter, best known for *Dixie* (1859). He formed the first troupe of black-face 'Negro Minstrels'.

Fillmore, Millard (1800–74), President of the United States (1850–53). He opposed intervention in foreign disputes and encouraged trading relations between Japan and the western world. He was presidential candidate of the Know-Nothing Party in 1856.

Foster, Stephen Collins (1826–64), songwriter. His best known songs include *My Old Kentucky Home, The Old Folks at Home* (1851) and *Jeanie with the Light Brown Hair*. They were adopted by the popular Negro minstrel groups of the time.

Franklin, Benjamin (1706–90), statesman, author, inventor and scientist. In Philadelphia he set up his own newspaper and annually produced *Poor Richard's Almanack* (1732–57). He invented the lightning rod in 1752. He served as a diplomat and was a signatory of the Declaration of Independence. His *Autobiography* was first published complete in 1868.

Freneau, Philip Morin (1752–1832), poet. He is best known for his political poems. His works include *A Poem on the Rising Glory of America* (1772) and *American Liberty* (1775). He also wrote of nature and the Indian in, e.g., *The Indian Burying Ground* (1788).

Garfield, James Abram (1831–81), President of the United States. Elected to the Presidency in 1880, he was shot in July, 1881, and died two months later.

Harte, Francis Brett (1836–1902), short-story writer, novelist, editor and poet, known as Bret Harte. His best known stories are *The Luck of Roaring Camp* (1868) and *The Outcasts of Poker Flat* (1869) which first appeared in *The Overland Monthly*, a magazine Harte edited from 1868 to 1870. His sentimental and humorous writing portrays thieves and vagabonds as more admirable than the law-abiding.

Harrison, Benjamin (1833–1901), President of the United States (1889–93). He approved the McKinley Tariff Act. Under his administration the first Pan-American Conference was held in 1889.

Hawthorne, Nathaniel (1804–64), novelist and short-story writer. In 1837 and 1842 he published *The Twice Told Tales*, a collection of tales and sketches. He was acquainted with Henry Wadsworth Longfellow and Herman Melville (*qq.v.*). His second collection, *Mosses from an Old Manse*, appeared in 1846. His novels include *The Scarlet Letter* (1850) and *The House of the Seven Gables* (1851).

Henry, O., pseudonym of William Sidney Porter (1862–1910), short-story writer. He is chiefly remembered for the humour of his writing and his use of the surprise ending. He served a term of imprisonment which provided material for many of his stories. All of his stories and some of his poems appeared in two volumes, *Works of O. Henry* (1953).

Henry, Patrick (1736–99), statesman and orator. He served in the Continental Congress and as Governor of Virginia.

Holmes, Oliver Wendell, Sr. (1809–94), physician, teacher and man of letters. His series, *The Autocrat of the Breakfast Table*, which appeared in *The Atlantic Monthly*, combined fiction, verse, drama, essay and conversation, and made Holmes famous for his wit and originality. His best known poems include *The Chambered Nautilus* (1858) and *The Deacon's Masterpiece* (1858).

Hopkinson, Joseph (1770–1842), jurist. In spite of a fairly distinguished legal career, he is chiefly remembered as the author of *Hail, Columbia* (1798).

Howe, Julia Ward (1819–1910), poet and reformer. She was particularly interested in female suffrage, prison reform and international peace. She wrote *The Battle Hymn of the Republic* (1862). Her collections of verse include *Passion Flowers* (1854).

Irving, Washington (1783–1859), essayist, biographer and historian. Under the pen-name of Diedrich Knickerbocker, he wrote the satirical *A History of New York . . .* (1809). His collection of tales and sketches, *The Sketch Book of Geoffrey Crayon, Gent.*, was published in Europe in 1820. His other works include *Bracebridge Hall* (1822), *The Conquest of Granada* (1829) and *A Tour on the Prairie* (1835).

Jackson, Andrew (1767–1845), President of the United States (1829–37). He served during the War of 1812 and is probably best remembered for the widening of presidential powers during his administration.

Jefferson, Thomas (1743–1826), President of the United States (1801–9). He drafted the Declaration of Independence with Benjamin Franklin (*q.v.*). While minister to France he published his *Notes on Virginia* (1784–5). He led the Democratic-Republican party and was vice-president to John Adams. The Louisiana Purchase occurred during his administration. His later works include *A Manual of Parliamentary Practice* (1801).

Key, Francis Scott (1779–1843), lawyer and poet. He wrote *The Star Spangled Banner*, which became the American national anthem by presidential order in 1916, confirmed by Congress in 1931.

Lazarus, Emma (1849–87), poet and translator. Her works include *Songs of a Semite* (1882) and a sonnet, *The New Colossus* (1883), which is inscribed on the pedestal of the Statue of Liberty.

Lincoln, Abraham (1809–65), President of the United States (1861–5). He studied law and was admitted to the bar in 1838. He served in Congress (1847–9), where he opposed the Mexican War. He won the Republican presidential nomination in 1860. The Civil War took place during his term of office. Lee had already surrendered when Lincoln was assassinated. Abraham Lincoln has become a major American folk hero.

Longfellow, Henry Wadsworth (1807–82), poet, translator and teacher of modern languages. His poetry enhanced his reputation at home and abroad, especially with such works as *The Village Blacksmith* and *The Song of Hiawatha* (1855). He introduced and translated a considerable amount of European literature to the U.S., notably Dante's *Divine Comedy*.

Lowell, James Russell (1819–91), poet, lawyer and teacher. He established his reputation with the satirical

Biglow Papers (1848, 1867), written in Yankee dialect. He was a professor at Harvard (1856–86) and editor of *The Atlantic Monthly* (1857–61) and *The North American Review* (1864–72). He served as a diplomat in Spain and England.

McCrae, John (1872–1918), Canadian poet and physician. He is best known for his poem *In Flanders Fields*, written during World War I.

McKinley, William (1843–1901), President of the United States (1897–1901). He sponsored the McKinley Tariff Act. The Spanish-American War was fought during his first term of office. He was assassinated in 1901.

Madison, James (1751–1836), President of the United States (1809–17). He was a member of the Constitutional Convention of 1787 and was influential in framing the U.S. Constitution. The War of 1812 was fought during his first term of office.

Melville, Herman (1819–91), novelist, short-story writer and poet. His experiences at sea and of life among cannibals inspired such works as *Typee: A Peep at Polynesian Life* (1846), *Omoo* (1847) and *Redburn* (1849). These were not simply straightforward adventure stories but had a high content of metaphysical symbolism. Melville's best known work is *Moby Dick: or, The White Whale* (1851), a symbolic study of good and evil. He later turned to writing poetry. It was not until long after his death that he was acknowledged as a great literary figure.

Paine, Thomas (1737–1809), writer and political pamphleteer. He was born in England and moved to America in 1774. His views were radical; he defended the American Revolution in *Common Sense* (1776) and *The American Crisis* (1776–83) and the French Revolution in *The Rights of Man* (1791; 1792). In 1792 he fled to Paris where he published *The Age of Reason* (1794; 1795) and *Letter to Washington* (1796). Although ostracized on his return to the U.S. in 1802, he subsequently came to be regarded as an American patriot.

Payne, John Howard (1791–1852), actor, playwright and poet. He established a formidable reputation as an actor in New York and in England before turning to dramatic writing. Among his works is *Clari, The Maid of Milan* (1823) and the comedy *Charles II* (published 1917), written with Washington Irving (*q.v.*).

Penn, William (1644–1718), English Quaker and founder of Pennsylvania. He named this land, granted by James II, in memory of his father. A liberal government allowed religious freedom and maintained friendly relations with the Indians. He wrote *Some Fruits of Solitude* (1693).

Pierpont, John (1785–1866), lawyer, clergyman and poet. He worked in the Treasury Department and published a few verses.

Pinkney, Edward Coote (1802–28), lawyer, teacher and poet, born in England. As he died at 26, his output of verse was not great.

Poe, Edgar Allen (1809–49), poet, critic and short-story writer. *Tamerlane and Other Poems* appeared in 1827 when Poe was only 18. The influence of the English Romantic poets can be seen in *Poems* (1831). In 1837 he began the serialization of *The Narrative of A. Gordon Pym*. Poe's most popular works have been his tales of mystery and horror, including *The Murders in the Rue Morgue* (1841) and *The Pit and the Pendulum* (1842).

Roosevelt, Theodore (1858–1919), President of the United States (1901–9). He wrote history before embarking on his political career. *The Naval War of 1812* appeared in 1882 and *Winning of the West* in four volumes in 1896–9. Roosevelt was elected Governor of New York in 1898 and became President on McKinley's death in 1901. He won the Nobel Peace Prize in 1906 and pressed for U.S. support for the Allies in World War I.

Saxe, John Godfrey (1816–87), lawyer and writer. He served as State Attorney in Vermont before entering journalism. His early works are mostly humorous, his later more melancholic.

Stowe, Harriet Beecher (1811–96), novelist. Anti-slavery, she was extremely interested and involved in religion. Her most famous work is *Uncle Tom's Cabin* (1852).

Thoreau, Henry David (1817–62), essayist, naturalist and poet. With his friend Ralph Waldo Emerson (*q.v.*) he was of the Transcendentalist group. Thoreau's best known work is *Walden* (1854), inspired by a stay in a remote log cabin. He believed that the simpler life is, the clearer its meaning becomes. His other works include *Cape Cod* and his *Journal* (1837–62).

Tompson, Benjamin (1642–1714), poet and teacher. He is credited with being the first native-born American to publish poetry in America. In 1676 he published *New England's Crisis*.

Twain, Mark, pseudonym of Samuel Langhorne Clemens (1835-1910), American author and humourist best known for novels recalling his youth by the Mississippi, *The Adventures of Tom Sawyer* (1876), *The Adventures of Huckleberry Finn* (1884). His reputation as a humourist originated from the tall-tale 'The Celebrated Jumping Frog of Calaveras County'. *Innocents Abroad* (1869) and *A Connecticut Yankee in King Arthur's Court* (1889) are amusing satires.

Ward, Artemus, pseudonym of Charles Farrar Browne (1834–67), humorist, editor and lecturer. Browne created, through his writings, the character of Ward, which became so widely known that author and creation merged. Ward was projected as an uneducated showman who wrote in Yankee dialect. The first collection was *Artemus Ward, His Book* (1862). In England he was editor of *Punch*. Other works include *Artemus Ward, His Travels* (1865) and *Artemus Ward's Lectures* (published 1869).

Washington, George (1732–99), first President of the United States (1789–97). He was a delegate to the Continental Congresses of 1774 and 1775, and commanded the Continental Army (1775) which was victorious at Princeton and Yorktown. During his administration he firmly established the authority of the new government.

Webster, Daniel (1782–1852), statesman and orator. He was elected to the Senate in 1827 and served as Secretary of State (1841–3).

Whitman, Walter (1819–92), poet, journalist and essayist. He was editor of the Brooklyn *Daily Eagle* (1846–7) and the Brooklyn *Freeman* (1848–9). His book of poems, *Leaves of Grass*, was published in 1855. Later editions (1856; 1892) were enlarged. Some of his best known poems, e.g. 'When Lilacs Last in the Dooryard Bloom'd', appeared in *Drum-Taps* (1865) and *Sequel to Drum-Taps* (1866).

Whittier, John Greenleaf (1807–92), poet and editor. He was a Quaker, committed to the cause of social reform, especially the abolition of slavery. His works include *Snow-Bound* and *The Barefoot Boy* (1855). His poem *Barbara Frietchie* (1863) was inspired by the Civil War.

Wigglesworth, Michael (1631–1705), poet and clergyman, born in England. *The Day of Doom* was published in 1662, and *Meat Out of the Eater* in 1669.

Wilcox, Ella Wheeler (1855–1919), poet. Collections of her work include *Poems of Passion* (1883) and *Poems of Pleasure* (1888).

Willis, Nathaniel Parker (1806–67), journalist and editor. He is best known for his moralistic poem *Unseen Spirits*, and a novel *Paul Vane* (1857).

Woodworth, Samuel (1784–1842), poet and playwright, best remembered for his play *The Forest Rose* and verse *The Old Oaken Bucket*.